D0734905

Wisdom from the Kitchen

Also by Sherry Conway Appel

From Mother to Daughter:
Advice and Lessons for a Good Life

Thanks, Mom

Wisdom from the Kitchen

From Mother to Daughter

Sherry Conway Appel

ST. MARTIN'S PRESS ❧ NEW YORK

WISDOM FROM THE KITCHEN: FROM MOTHER TO DAUGHTER.
Copyright © 1998 by Allen Appel and Sherry Conway Appel. All
rights reserved. Printed in the United States of America. No
part of this book may be used or reproduced in any manner
whatsoever without written permission except in the case of
brief quotations embodied in critical articles or reviews. For
information, address St. Martin's Press, 175 Fifth Avenue,
New York, N.Y. 10010.

Library of Congress Cataloging-in-Publication Data

Appel, Sherry Conway.
    Wisdom from the kitchen: from mother to daughter / Sherry
Conway Appel.—1st St. Martin's Press ed.
        p. cm.
    ISBN 0-312-18099-3
    1. Cookery. 2. Food—Quotations, maxims, etc. 3. Cookery—
Quotations, maxims, etc. 4. Women—Quotations, maxims, etc.
I. Title.
TX714.A63   1998
641.5—dc21   97-39801
                                                            CIP

First Edition: April 1998

10 9 8 7 6 5 4 3 2 1

Books are available in quantity for promotional or premium use.
Write to Director of Special Sales, St. Martin's Press, 175 Fifth
Avenue, New York, N.Y. 10010, for information on discounts
and terms, or call toll-free (800) 221-7945. In New York, call
(212) 674-5151 (ext. 645).

In loving memory of the women who worked in kitchens before air conditioning and microwaves

For my mom, of course, but also for my dear mother-in-law, Irene Trippett Appel. May my daughter Leah learn much from these stories.

Introduction

A few weeks ago, I was peeling potatoes at the kitchen sink when my thirteen-year-old daughter came in, sat down, and began to fill me in on the day's events. I suddenly realized that this was a scene from my own childhood, when the yellow Formica table was the center of our family's life and my mother its heart. Coming home from school, I would walk through the back porch, grab a bottle of cream soda from the crate, and run into the kitchen, a big airy room filled with sunshine. Just-baked banana bread or maybe some chocolate chip cookies would be waiting on the daisy plate. And Mother would be waiting, too. I would sit down and we'd talk.

She'd usually be peeling potatoes or cleaning greens, getting ready for the next meal. With five kids, she had plenty to prepare, but I never once heard her complain. In fact, she took enormous pride and interest in cooking for us—she was always trying new recipes she found in *Better Homes and Gardens, McCall's*, or the newspaper. Our meals were hearty—always meat, lots of potatoes, vegetables, and usually a salad, which she had perfected to an art. She wasn't an ethnic cook; I often envied some of my friends for their families' heritage and their kielbasa, hlupki, or pasta. We were pretty much anchored in the mainstream fifties with meatloaf, pot roast, and chicken and dumplings as staples.

My mother also loved to entertain. My father was an army colonel, and she was often called upon to hold receptions and large gatherings in our home for the officers. Preparation for the parties would go on for days. My oldest sister baked special rolls for the ham, and Mom would make a million lilliputian meatballs and cheese pastries. And the desserts!

Mom's chocolate eclairs, brownies, pecan tassies, and little cheesecakes would all be arranged just so on plates with lace doilies.

My mother's focus in life was her family—her husband and her children. Her role was to provide the stable center; the center from which we all spun out our lives. And she loved it—relished it as much as she did her weekly bridge game and bowling league.

My life is much different from hers. We eat out and carry in a lot more often. I have a full-time job so I am not there when my children get home from school. But I still make sure to have those cookies or pie or some other baked good on hand for them. Baking is my mother's legacy to me, along with eating dinner together as a family in the dining room every evening, making chocolate pudding for an after-dinner snack, and creating the best chocolate soda you ever tasted.

My last vivid memory of my mother was in the kitchen of my new house. My parents had come for a visit, bringing as they often did a rib roast and rutabaga. We were cooking dinner and my mother was giving me the details of some new dish she had discovered. She was dancing, the light was behind her, highlighting her blonde, near-white hair, a joyful smile on her face. She was beautiful.

1

In the Kitchen with Mom

Always, always, always wash your hands!

All of the interesting things at our house happened in the kitchen. If there was a roar of laughter, it came through the kitchen doors. If there was a fight or a reconciliation, it happened in the kitchen. Despite my mother's continual attempts to limit the number of cooks in the kitchen, everyone knew that's where the action was.
—*Stephanie Benkovic*

In our house the kitchen was the warmest room. We lived on a farm and in the winter the heat was turned off at night. In the morning Mom would get up early and turn on the oven and open the oven door. We'd dash downstairs with our clothes in our arms and dress in front of the stove. Mom would make our breakfast as we dressed. It was a warm, happy way to start the day.

—*Sally Reister*

Buy a basic cookbook, like The Joy of Cooking, *and start there if you're just learning. You can move up to the gourmet stuff later.*

Don't store your spices over the stove. The heat robs them of their strength.

Keep your coffee, beans or grind, in the freezer.

Make sure your tap water doesn't taste like minerals or chlorine before you make coffee with it. Your best bet is to use bottled water.

If you're running late, set the table and start cooking an onion. When your family gets home, they'll think you've been cooking all day.

I grew up in a family with an older brother and a twin sister. We loved when our mother made one particular roll, which we requested on every special occasion. We continue to request them, though we have long since moved away and only come home for visits. We like them so much we named them "Dear Little Rolls."

—*Elizabeth Force Carson*

Dear Little Rolls

COMBINE AND COOL:
1 cup milk, scalded
$1/2$ cup margarine
$1/2$ cup sugar
1 teaspoon salt

ADD:
1 package dry yeast
3 beaten eggs

Add the above ingredients to $4^1/2$ cups flour. Mix until ingredients form a smooth, soft dough. Knead lightly on floured surface for several minutes. Place dough in greased bowl. Cover. Let rise until at least double in bulk.

Divide dough in thirds; roll each third out on floured surface to 9-inch circle. Brush with melted butter. Cut each circle in 12 to 16 wedges. Roll each wedge starting with wide end. Arrange on greased baking sheet and brush with melted butter. Cover and let rise until almost double in size.

Bake at 400°F for 10 to 15 minutes. Remove rolls from pan and brush with butter and cool on racks.

My mother is many things, but the only thing she ever did well in the kitchen was talk on the phone!
—*Karyn Lynch*

Whenever my mother would write to me, she would throw in a recipe. Once it was for split pea soup, another time for a lasagna that caught her eye. My mother's handwriting resembled an ant crawling across the page, so it was always a challenge to decipher what was written. I've kept her letters and recipes; when I read them I hear her voice, and remember how much she cared for me.
—*Sherry Conway Appel*

2

Comfort Food

$\mathcal{I}$ can still remember the day when I was sick with the mumps. I was seven years old and my throat hurt, and my glands were swollen. My mom had tucked me in on the sofa, with a big pillow and blanket; I had a book of Pogo comics to read. On the TV table next to me was a glass of ginger ale and a box of Kleenex. At lunchtime she came in with a cup of tomato soup, a grilled cheese sandwich, and a big bowl of chocolate pudding.

Forty years later when I'm feeling lonely or blue or just plain tired from the rush of life, I reach for that same comfort food to get me through. I don't have my mother anymore, but I still feel the comfort and love she gave me through those special foods she made.

—*Sherry Conway Appel*

The best way to make grilled cheese sandwiches is to spread the butter on the bread before putting it in the pan. You can toss a chunk of butter in the pan and swirl it around but it just won't be as good.

Whenever I spent the night at my grandmother's house, she and I always made Creamettes, her version of macaroni and cheese. This was her favorite comfort food (although there was no such term in her day), and came to be both my mother's and mine as well. We both still make it whenever we are feeling low.

—*Lynn Gutter*

Grandma Sophie's Macaroni and Cheese

To make Creamettes, you boil as much elbow macaroni as you can eat. In a skillet, melt enough butter to coat the pan. When the skillet is hot, add the cooked macaroni and several large chunks of cream cheese. Stir and reduce the heat to very low, and cover until cream cheese is soft and melted. Stir macaroni until well coated with cream cheese. Season with salt and pepper. Put on your pajamas and your robe, serve macaroni in a nice bowl, eat.

What's a kugel? A noodle casserole just doesn't have quite the right sound, but it's a close approximation. When it's warm, it's just wonderful. The aroma is heavenly, the taste divine, and it feels like your Mom's arms are around you keeping you safe from all the world's evils.

—*Beverly Silverberg*

Grandmother's Kugel (noodle pudding)

1 16-ounce package broad egg noodles
3 large apples (Granny Smiths or comparable)
3 eggs, separated
½ cup raisins
½ cup sugar
Lots of cinnamon
Pinch of salt
1 stick butter (margarine if you must)

Boil the noodles (don't overcook). Pare and dice the apples and mix them with the noodles. Beat the egg yolks and add the raisins, sugar, cinnamon, and salt. Pour over the noodles and stir gently to distribute. With a little of the butter, grease a Pyrex dish large enough to hold the noodles. Cut up the rest of the butter and mix with the noodles. Whip the egg whites until stiff and gently fold into mixture. Pour into baking dish and bake at 350°F for 30 minutes or until golden.

Always heat the milk you use to make mashed potatoes. The microwave works fine for this job.

Always start bacon in a cold pan.

It never works to just turn up the heat to make things cook faster, that way you just burn the food.

When I was a little girl, my mother always took the time to make me feel special when I was sick. Usually I wasn't interested in eating so her challenge was to get some food into me.

Mother would bring me my food on a tray, beautifully decorated with flowers and a cloth napkin tucked in a napkin ring. Then she would begin to "weave a tale" about the food. My favorite was "The Hungry Frog." You guessed it. I was the frog.

The meal was arranged to resemble a small pond. Grits with a pool of butter in the middle were garnished with a hard-boiled egg sliced in wedges and placed in the butter. The egg was the lily in the pond. The pepper shaker was on the tray ready to sprinkle "bugs" if the frog so wished.

I use my mother's idea to "weave a tale" with my own children. Trucks for Bill, and ballerinas and bunnies for his friend Mary Beth. These "make-believe" lunches always leave an empty plate!

—*Jane G. Kelly*

When we didn't feel especially well or on a cold winter's night, baked custards always seemed to hit the spot. Even now, I make it for my own family on a winter evening. The recipe was passed from Jane Carolyn Fleming to Dorothy V. Fleming and then to me. It is now a part of the recipe box I give to my daughters at their wedding showers.

When this custard cools, it has a baked custard top and a heavier cakelike custard layer on the bottom. It was a favorite with all Grandmother's children and their families. Now that she has passed away, it always brings me fond memories of her when I bake it.

—*Anne Ridgely*

Old-Fashioned Custard

Grease a black cast-iron skillet. (I use vegetable spray.)

Stir until well blended (a wire whisk works well):

4 well-beaten eggs
½ cup sugar
2 teaspoons vanilla
1 quart milk
1 cup flour (enough to make a cakelike batter)

Pour into skillet. Bake at 350°F to 375°F for about 1 hour or until a knife inserted into the center comes out clean.

3
Everyday Cooking

IT ALL STARTS WITH A JAR OF TOMATOES

As a little girl growing up, I thought everyone had a summer vegetable garden. My mom and Aunt Mary had an unspoken race to see who would have the first ripe tomato. My mother insisted I help with weeding and hilling the tomatoes. I never cared much for ripe tomatoes and I hated working in the garden.

In August the tomatoes were ready to be canned. Tomato canning was a lot of work. The tomatoes were washed and covered with boiling water to loosen the skins. We sat for what seemed like hours, peeling and coring the tomatoes on the back porch. At this point, my mom took over. Canning was very serious business and there could be no mistakes. It had to be perfect. Mother told me horror stories of families being poisoned because *the mother* was not careful when she canned.

After the jars were filled and processed, they were moved to the canning section of the basement, and covered with newspapers. I don't think Mom could have slept without her 300 jars of canned tomatoes.

When I got to junior high, I started to cook. Our recipes were very simple. START WITH A JAR OF TOMATOES. Chili—start with a jar of tomatoes. Spaghetti sauce—start with a jar of tomatoes. Vegetable soup—start with a jar of tomatoes. And of course, one of my very favorites—breaded tomatoes.

I cried the first three times I wrote this, but I enjoyed doing it.

—*Anna Rae Ruckman*

Breaded Tomatoes

1 jar of home-canned tomatoes
1 tablespoon flour
1 teaspoon sugar
¼ cup milk
2 cups broken day-old bread

While heating the tomatoes, stir in the tablespoon of flour. After it has thickened slightly, stir in the sugar, milk, and chunks of bread. Serve when hot.

If you want to please your husband soon after you get married, ask his mother what his favorite foods are and how to cook them. That way you can make the best from his family and the best from yours.

In making chicken soup, use kosher chickens— they're more flavorful. Also, add dill at the very end. If you add it too early, it leaves a bitter taste in the soup.

My sisters and I learned to cook on a coal stove. We also had a real icebox that held chunks of ice. It had a special wire cage in which you put food you wanted to protect from the mice.

—*Eileen Toumonoff*

If you're boiling eggs and one or more have cracks in the shell, put a teaspoon of salt in the water. This will keep the white from leaking out.

Add a teaspoon or so of water when you're making scrambled eggs. The liquid breaks up the whites and yolks and gives a finer consistency.

My kids hate it when their cereal is not very crisp. I put it in the oven at 350 degrees for two or three minutes and it crisps right up.

When I was growing up, my mom, Martha Dawson, used to make salmon loaf for dinner. It was my job to take the little backbones and skin off the canned salmon before she mixed the ingredients.

After I was married, I copied the recipe for myself and used it often with my family. One day I went to use the recipe and couldn't find it anywhere. I looked in my card box and in all the recipe books but it was gone. I couldn't call my mom because she had passed away. Eventually I gave up looking and forgot about it.

Then one day I was in my craft room looking for something else and found it in with other little treasures I had saved while cleaning up. I stopped what I was doing and remembered my mom. I knew she must have been looking down on me that day.

—*Barbara Dawson Marcinko*

Salmon Loaf

2 eggs
1 pound can red salmon
3 slices soft bread, cubed
1 teaspoon salt
¼ cup margarine, melted
1½ cups milk

Beat eggs until light. Drain salmon, remove skin and bones, and then flake. Add beaten eggs and bread, salt, and margarine. Heat milk to lukewarm. Add to salmon mixture. Mix thoroughly. Place in a greased loaf pan and bake at 350°F for one hour.

Put a pinch of sugar in the cooking water when you're making Lima beans.

A little salt on grapefruit makes it taste sweeter.

It is a myth that you can tell how ripe a pineapple is by easily pulling out the leaves in the center.

My mother's prowess in the kitchen was insubstantial; and there was little variety in what she served. To her credit, Neva Gan was stalwart in her preparation of the few dishes she did fix. She never failed to send me and my brother off to school with a good breakfast. Every morning we had bacon, a fried egg, and toast. (This was the fifties. No one had heard of fat and cholesterol.) Mother's fried eggs became famous among my friends who were treated to them on weekend mornings after sleepovers. My soul mate, Lucy, occasionally cooks eggs my mother's way now and her family calls them "Mrs. Weeks's Eggs."

This is my mother's recipe: Give your children latitude, don't flip your eggs, and if your husband wants to cook, let him.

—*Mary Dail*

Mrs. Weeks's Eggs

After frying bacon, remove pan from the heat to allow the grease to cool somewhat. Crack the egg into a dish. Then slide the egg carefully into the pan of bacon grease so as not to break the yolk. Return pan to medium-low heat. Using a spatula, gently and repeatedly sweep the grease over the egg until the yolk reaches the desired doneness. The result is an egg that has never been flipped but is cooked to perfection, with no crispy edges or crunchy undersides. The final touch, and Mother's only bit of kitchen eclecticism, is to season the egg lightly with white pepper.

Cooking cabbage can make the house smell. Put a piece of bread in the pot and this will cut down on the smell. This also works for cauliflower.

If hard cheese is a little moldy, cut that part off. It won't hurt anything. If soft cheese is moldy, throw it out.

Clean the sink out after poultry.

If you can smell Brussels sprouts or broccoli, you've probably overcooked them.

Mom's blueberry muffins have been a hit for years. The secret is to mix lightly just until the ingredients are moistened. When I had a shower luncheon, or had to take something to a pot luck, I always made Mom's blueberry muffins. Everyone wanted the recipe. Now when I go places, I can't tell you how many times I hear, "I made your mom's blueberry muffins and thought of you." It always brings a smile to my face, as I think of my mother.

—*Susan Conway Himes*

Blueberry Muffins

1 cup blueberries
1½ cups sifted flour
½ cup sugar
2 teaspoons baking powder
½ teaspoon salt
¼ cup shortening
1 egg
½ cup milk

Wash blueberries and dry. Sift dry ingredients. Cut in shortening until it resembles coarse crumbs. Add egg and milk and stir just until blended. (Do not over-stir.) Add blueberries. Drop batter into greased muffin tins. Bake at 400°F for 16 to 20 minutes. Yield: 12 muffins.

To keep the bottoms of muffins from getting soggy, let them cool a minute in the pan and then run a knife around them and pop them out. Put them upside-down on a plate and let them cool until they are ready to eat.

If muffins are stuck in the pan, set it on a wet towel for a few minutes.

Salting dried beans as they cook makes them tough. Always salt after they're finished cooking. The same is true with making scrambled eggs. Always add the salt after cooking, not during.

In my Italian neighborhood, I grew up thinking we were all related. Family meant food to my mother, and good meals were her trademark. We hardly ever went out because restaurant food of any price and caliber could not compare to her dishes.

It must have been hard work to cook so many meals, but my mother was never taken for granted. We all lavished praise on her, and loved her very much. There was no shyness in our family, so we said what we thought or felt, and we said it out loud!

—*Ann P. Cochran*

Tomato Sauce

2 large onions, chopped
6 large cloves garlic, chopped
¾ cup olive oil
2 large cans (28 ounce) tomatoes, pureed
1 tablespoon each oregano and basil
½ tablespoon each salt and pepper
1 teaspoon sugar
2 small cans tomato paste

In a large pot, brown onion and garlic in olive oil. Add pureed tomatoes, and then add the seasonings. Simmer 1 hour. Add 2 cans tomato paste and 4 of water. Cook for a second hour. If you are adding meat of any kind, add it after the first hour.

Meatballs

¾ pound ground beef
¼ pound ground pork
¾ cup bread crumbs
¼ teaspoon garlic powder
5 tablespoons grated Parmesan cheese
1 tablespoon minced parsley
2 eggs, beaten
1 teaspoon salt
¼ teaspoon pepper

Combine all ingredients. With damp hands, roll mixture into balls. Coat pan with oil (a spray-on product today!) and place on pan. Bake at 350°F for 45 minutes.

Never put a cover on the pot when you're boiling green beans. It makes them lose their color.

How to cook fresh corn on the cob: Bring a pot of water to boil and put in fresh corn. When it comes back to a boil, put the lid on, turn off the stove, and move the pot off the burner. Wait five minutes and eat.

If cornsilk is hard to get off, rub the ears with a damp paper towel.

If you're cooking liver and you think it's going to be tough, soak it in milk for an hour and then fry it in butter.

My grandmother's house in Karachi, Pakistan, was my extended family home. Although we are now scattered around the globe, we are still very close. We all make an effort to get together there every two years. And you can be sure that we never eat out during this time. Everyone pitches in, not just to help with cooking for a crowd, but also to refresh and fine-tune our recipe memories.

Although I have the technique down for my mother's recipes, I can never replicate hers in taste. As our favorite saying goes, "The taste is in the touch of the cook's hand."

—*Rabia Khan*

Daal (lentils)

This is a fool-proof method of making lentils. You can add more vegetables, puree the end result, and turn this into a hearty winter soup. Daal is also great served with rice, nan bread, or even a slice of toast in the middle of the night. You can freeze this as soon as it is cooked and it will stay in your freezer for up to a week. Take out individual servings to reheat.

2 teaspoons vegetable oil
3 cloves garlic, crushed
1 cup red lentils, washed and soaked in water for
    about an hour
1 teaspoon salt
2 medium tomatoes, diced
½ cup coriander leaves
1 medium onion, peeled and left whole
¼ cup lemon juice
½ teaspoon chili powder
½ teaspoon turmeric powder

Heat oil in a quart saucepan. Add garlic and stir for about 2 minutes. Drain the lentils and add to saucepan. Cook while stirring for about 3 minutes until the oil is absorbed by the lentils. Add salt and enough water to cover up to an inch above the level of the lentils. Cook on medium heat until the water evaporates down to the level of the lentils. Add the remainder of the ingredients and enough water to comfortably cover all the ingredients. Simmer on low heat until most of the liquid evaporates and the consistency of your choice is reached. The lentils will disintegrate. The onion should stay whole throughout the cooking process and can be cut into individual servings for the meal. Garnish with more chopped coriander.

You can hold rice on the stove top for up to half an hour without harm as long as you don't take the top off. This gives you a margin of error when you're timing your cooking schedule.

Never try to cook risotto or paella with any rice except Italian arborio, which is sold in most grocery stores these days. Any other rice breaks apart in the process.

As a teen in the days before many electrical appliances, I helped in the kitchen but didn't like to mash potatoes. Mom wanted to have them mashed while she made the gravy. I would grumble. She would say, "You mash the potatoes and I will save enough to make potato cakes." It is easy to do. Just add an egg to the leftover potatoes and stir in some flour to reach the right consistency. Roll patties in flour and put in a very hot greased skillet until they are brown on each side. I'm past age seventy now and still love potato cakes. They conjure up memories of a warm kitchen and a fun-filled home.

—*Peggy Cavender*

Use ground chuck when making hamburgers. If you remove all the fat while cooking (tilt the pan and spoon it out) the burgers end up being no fattier than the leaner, more expensive types.

Don't oversqueeze the meat when making hamburgers. Use a light touch.

Baked potatoes just aren't as good cooked in a microwave. If you're short on time, however, microwave them for five minutes or so, then bake for twenty or thirty minutes.

We come from hardy Pennsylvania Dutch stock where food "sticks to your ribs." This recipe was never written down, only verbally passed along, but it is quite delicious with a variety of foods. My Grandma Fissel was adamant about proportions with this recipe: "You must always double your sugar to your vinegar or it won't turn out right."

This dressing can be served over any salad greens or fresh spinach, adding hard-cooked eggs, fresh mushrooms, feta cheese, and croutons. It is also good on cooked cabbage. Boil bite-size chunks of cabbage until limp, drain liquid, and add hot dressing to pan. Stir well before serving.

—*Nancy Fissel Hauser*

Hot Bacon Dressing

8 slices bacon
2 eggs
1 cup sugar
½ cup cider vinegar

Fry the bacon until crisp and remove from the pan. Meanwhile beat eggs with a fork in a bowl and add sugar. Stir until smooth, then stir in the vinegar. Cool bacon grease. (I remove all but approximately 2 to 3 tablespoons of the grease in the frying pan.) Slowly add egg, sugar, and vinegar mixture to grease. Over high heat, stir constantly until mixture bubbles and thickens. Reduce heat and simmer. Crumble bacon into dressing and add chopped onion, if desired.

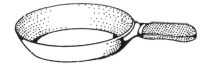

4

Sunday Dinner, Big Meals, and Leftovers

*R*oast chicken was always a real standby in our house. It seemed like my mother could stretch one chicken out for three or four meals. What I looked forward to the most was the creamed chicken on biscuits that came the night after the roast chicken. There were lots of fluffy buttermilk biscuits and plenty of creamy gravy to go on them. My biscuits aren't as good as my mom's, even though I use the same recipe. But put enough chicken and gravy on them, and they'll do just fine. There's no cream in creamed chicken, we just call it that.

—*Irene Appel*

Creamed Chicken on Biscuits

Evening #1. Roast a chicken. Get one with the pop-up thermometer; the directions are on the package. The secret is to make enough gravy so that you have plenty for the first night and enough left over for the creamed chicken part. Spoon off all but a couple of tablespoons of fat after roasting, blend in three tablespoons of flour, then add at least one can of chicken broth and enough liquid to total three cups. If you need to add more flour to thicken, do so, being careful to break up the lumps.

    Evening #2. Put leftover gravy in a pan and set the heat to low. While the gravy melts, pick what's left of the chicken off the carcass, and cut into small, bite-size pieces. Put them in the gravy. Heat just to boiling, being careful that it doesn't burn, which it is likely to do if you're not watching. Pour it over the biscuits and eat.

Always keep a warm place in your heart for your freezer. When making that favorite dish, double or triple it, label it, date it, and freeze it! You'll love yourself and the microwave-ready dish on those "days from hell."

—*Ruth Rice Crone*

Rub your chicken all over with soy sauce before roasting. It gives it a lovely brown color.

Make sure the butter you use in your biscuits is cold before you cut it in. And don't overwork the dough or you'll get tough biscuits.

My grandmother, who I called Nana, made wonderful brisket. One Sunday, I had an urge for brisket, so I called Nana and asked her for the recipe. By then she was in her late eighties. She gave me the recipe and then asked me when I was going to serve it. When I told her I planned to serve it that evening she was appalled! She told me that brisket needs to be cooked in two stages over two days. The first time, I prepared it in one day. Every time since then, I have prepared it over two days, and she was right—it is best that way. Here's the recipe the way she gave it to me.

—*Liz McClain*

Nana's Brisket

Take a nice lean piece of brisket—first cut. Brown it in a very hot skillet with salt and pepper. Add lots of sliced onions and chopped garlic. Once browned, add a little liquid (water, stock, or wine) and one small can of tomato sauce. Cover and put in a 325°F oven for two hours. Remove from the oven and take the brisket out of the sauce, wrap in aluminum foil, and refrigerate. Put the sauce in a container and refrigerate. The next day, slice the brisket very thin, put it in a pan, and pour the sauce over it. Cover and bake at 300°F for one hour.

If you burn the dinner rolls on the bottom, scrape off the burned part with your kitchen grater.

Roasts with bones are always more flavorful than those without.

Don't put a roast straight from the refrigerator directly into the oven. It needs to sit out for two or three hours, if possible. And don't serve a roast directly from the oven. It needs to rest for twenty minutes or so before being served.

Roast your beef in a shallow pan. It will brown better.

Salt meat after you cook it, not before.

Every Sunday, my grandmothers and aunts and uncles came over for dinner. We'd all gather around the dining room table, set with the good china, fancy glasses, tablecloth, and napkins. No one was in a hurry. We'd share time with one another, a good meal, and, of course, Mom's dinner rolls. How I loved them! She would allow me to make my whole meal out of her yummy rolls, butter, and jelly. The grace she allowed me probably has something to do with my great fondness for bread products that exists to this day!

—Linda O'Connor

Set the oven racks to the proper height before you preheat the oven, not after.

Never throw out a ham bone. Freeze it and use it when making beans or greens.

I cook greens, collards or kale, by washing, chopping, and then sautéing or steaming them for about five minutes in a large pot with a little olive oil and some chopped garlic. My mom makes hers by putting a ham bone and a couple of inches of water in a large pot on the stove and gently boiling the ham bone for an hour. Then she puts in the chopped greens and cooks them for around twenty or thirty minutes. Mine taste good and are probably healthier, but hers are better.

—*Annie Felts*

Always use at least three changes of water when washing greens.

Using freshly ground peppercorns is always better than the already-ground variety.

It's all right to use canned chicken broth.

My mother always had a three-day rule for leftovers. After three days if it's still in there, toss it out. It's a good rule; I wish I followed it.
—*Amanda Fredrickson*

5

Entertaining

$\mathcal{I}$'m reminded of the cocktail parties my parents used to have when we were kids. Remember how green olives used to be everywhere? In the martinis, on the relish tray, sitting around impaled on toothpicks, wrapped with bacon or cheese and baked. We kids would always suck out the pimento and put them on our fingers as fancy grown-up rings or little puppets. We could never figure out how our parents could stand them. Now we know that if you wrap a martini around them they taste just fine.

—*Sandy Fisher*

People love to help in the kitchen. Give them some simple job like chopping celery to keep them out of the way and they'll be happy.

The general rule "You get what you pay for" is usually true when buying wine. Don't demean a great meal with cheap wine.

When opening champagne, put a clean kitchen towel over the bottle top and ease the cork out by twisting it back and forth slowly. That business of blasting out the cork and having the champagne spill all over the floor is a waste and amusing only to people who have already had too much to drink.

When "plumping" raisins, use rum as the liquid. Let the raisins soak in the rum (Meyer's dark is the best). When the raisins are ready, use them in your recipe and drink the raisin-scented rum.

My parents met while working in the 5th General Army Hospital in Germany. My mom was a civilian nurse and my dad was an army pharmacist. On dates they would have fondue. When they came back to the states, they brought the recipe with them. The first Valentine's Day after I got married, they gave me a fondue pot complete with the recipe. It is a fun meal to share with lots of friends. A German and Swiss tradition is that if you lose your bread in the fondue, you have to kiss all the men/women at the table!

—*Julie Himes Gerig*

Cheese Fondue

1 to 3 cloves garlic
1 cup good dry white wine
1½ tablespoons flour
1½ pounds of shredded Gruyere and Emmenthaler
    cheese (combined)
2½ tablespoons Kirsch
Salt and pepper to taste
Good bread, Italian or French round, cut into cubes

Rub garlic on inside of double boiler or heavy fondue pan. Heat white wine. Toss flour and cheese together before adding to wine/garlic mixture. Melt cheese mixture in wine, stirring in figure-eight formation with wooden spoon. Before transferring to fondue pot or fondue base, stir in Kirsch, salt, and pepper. Serve with bread for dipping.

Candles make culinary sins invisible, while providing warmth and romance.
                    —*Carolyn Crone*

6

Holidays

There are two kinds of Jewish holidays—Eating and Not Eating. For Passover you've got your seder dinner; there's Break Fast after Yom Kippur, which is usually appetizers; Rosh Hashanah (New Year's) means lots of sweet stuff, which assures that the whole new year will be sweet. As a family of chopped liver lovers we used to find just about any excuse to have this particular dish and made it part of the fare at every Jewish holiday whether the occasion commemorated the new year or a tree-planting. Even somebody's birthday would do. Although we prepare it less often now because of its lofty height on the cholesterol Richter scale, this is one of my most-beloved "Mom" recipes.

—*Cina Radler*

Harriet's Chopped Liver

1 pound chicken livers
2 tablespoons oil
2 medium-to-large onions, diced
1/2 teaspoon onion salt
1/4 teaspoon garlic salt or powder
4 hard-boiled eggs
2 tablespoons mayonnaise
Dash pepper

Soak livers in a bowl of cold water. Peel off membranes and cut out veins. Dry livers on towel. In large frying pan, heat oil until smoking and add liver and onions. Sauté on medium-low until onions are golden and livers are cooked. Dump liver and onions into a wooden chopping bowl. Chop like crazy (finely) with metal hand chopper. Mix in seasonings. Mash eggs separately, then add to liver mixture. Add mayonnaise 1 tablespoon at a time; you might need 2 tablespoons. Taste to see if you need another 1/2 teaspoon onion salt. Refrigerate. Yield: One pound. Best if eaten cold.

On Christmas Eve, the Italian Catholic tradition is to have thirteen different kinds of fish for dinner—twelve for the apostles, and the last for Jesus. My mother-in-law Mary followed this tradition exactly. But by the time the grandchildren came along, she made less. Still, she'd have dried cod she'd soak for a week in the garage (changing the water every day) to use in making the tomato sauce. She'd have shrimp sautéed in garlic and butter, tuna antipasto, squid stuffed with bread crumbs, parsley, and pecans. Along with this would be fried cauliflower, roasted peppers, stuffed celery, and rice croquettes to go along with the sauce and spaghetti, as well as bread. After all, how much could you eat?

Although both Mary and her husband Dominic are gone, we still carry on the tradition. My husband and I make the old food in the traditional way, and we always have all the family over. It's a lot of work but a tradition I hope will continue after us.

—*Barbara Conway Abbruzzese*

Squid Stuffed with Bread Crumbs, Parsley, and Pecans

2 pounds squid
1 cup parsley, chopped
2 tablespoons Parmesan cheese
2 tablespoons bread crumbs
1 tablespoon garlic, minced
3 tablespoons pecans or pine nuts, chopped
Salt and pepper
Olive oil

Clean squid; cut off tentacles and reserve, clean interior, and remove clear cartilage in body. Sauté minced garlic for a minute or so and mix together with cup of chopped parsley, Parmesan cheese, bread crumbs, chopped pine nuts or pecans. Salt and pepper and moisten the mixture with olive oil.

Stuff mixture into body of squid (a baby spoon works best) about 2/3 full and secure the opening with a toothpick. Sauté stuffed squid and reserved tentacles in 4 tablespoons olive oil or olive oil and butter for approximately three or four minutes.

Squid can also be cooked in tomato sauce and served over pasta. In sauce, cook for at least thirty minutes.

Squid must be cooked for either a little time or a lot of time. Anything in between makes it tough.

This is actually my mom's next-door neighbor's recipe, but we didn't know that when we started calling it Grandma's Salad. She's a grandma, too, so I guess it still counts. We've heard it called Watergate Salad as well, but maybe they stole it from some grandma somewhere.

It's one of those concoctions that comes out of cans and containers and most of our fancy friends would never deign to make it. But at dinners most of those same friends keep on filling their bowls. Everybody loves Grandma's Salad. We serve it as part of every Thanksgiving and Christmas meal.

—*Sandy Fisher*

Grandma's Salad

Mix one package of instant pistachio pudding with 1 16-ounce can crushed pineapple. Add one container of Cool Whip. Add 1 16-ounce can of fruit cocktail, drained, and 2 small cans of mandarin oranges, one can drained, the other with juice. Sprinkle toasted hazelnuts on top. Chill before serving.

Learn to cook for yourself, your family, and your friends. Cooking is love.

Never try anything fancy for Thanksgiving. People don't want surprises, they want tradition.

My mom, Peggy Hale McCoy, was the best cook in town. She prepared food for her family and friends with a huge helping of love. Of all her delicious recipes, the one that brings back most vividly the memory of Mom in her kitchen is her recipe for caramel nut cookies, our traditional Christmas cookie. The spicy fragrance of those cookies baking would scent the house for two days. She didn't bake them just for her family, but for others as well. I don't know the origin of this recipe; it dates back at least to the 1940s when as a little girl I first began helping to decorate them. My father, my brother, and I would deliver them to friends and neighbors on Christmas Eve before church. These cookies are still my favorite. Christmas wouldn't be the same without them.

—*Sally McCoy Games*

Mom's Caramel-Nut Cookies

1 cup butter or margarine
2 cups dark brown sugar
2 eggs, beaten
1 teaspoon vanilla
$\frac{1}{2}$ cup sour cream
$\frac{1}{4}$ teaspoon salt
2 teaspoons cinnamon
1 teaspoon cloves
1 cup pecans, chopped
4 cups sifted flour
1 teaspoon baking soda
1 cup white raisins or shredded coconut (optional)

Cream butter and sugar. Add eggs, vanilla, and sour cream and beat two minutes. Combine spices and nuts with sifted flour and baking soda. Add to butter mixture. Fold in raisins or coconut if desired. Drop batter from the end of a teaspoon onto a greased cookie sheet. Decorate as you like with tinted coconut, cherries, pecan halves, or sugar crystals. Bake 12 minutes at 350°F. Yield: 5 dozen.

If you're using raw apples in a dish and they're over the hill or just plain bland, dust them with cinnamon or nutmeg.

My mom made corned beef and cabbage every year for St. Patrick's Day, even though we weren't Irish and we lived in the South. It seemed like pretty exotic food to us and though we loved it, no one ever thought to have it any other time of the year. It makes the best potatoes you can cook.

—*Lennie Doak*

Corned Beef and Cabbage

Buy one of those briskets already corned in the bag. The eye of round has a lot less fat but it doesn't cook up as tender. Put it in a pot and just cover with water. Open a beer, take a drink, and dump the rest in the pot. Bring to a boil, cover loosely, and cook for 2½ hours. Peel potatoes and put in with the beef and cook for 20 minutes. Cut a cabbage into 8 wedges and put in the pot and cook for another 10 minutes. Serve vegetables in a bowl with a little of the pot liquor. Cut meat against the grain into slices about a quarter to a half an inch thick. If it falls apart, don't worry, that means it's cooked just right.

My grandparents came from Czechoslovakia. My mom died when I was nine years old so my grandmother and aunt were my role models for cooking. My grandmother was in her eighties and couldn't speak English very well but was a great cook. She came over twice a week to help out. My aunt would come every evening and prepare dinner for us. Then her husband and son would join us and we would all eat together. We were lucky to have such a warm and loving extended family.

One of my last vivid memories of my mother was related to cooking. She was in the hospital, and I wanted to be her little helper. Someone had decided we were going to have fried chicken for dinner, so I started by heating the grease. I must have done something wrong, because I was burned badly on the face. We had to go and visit my mother that evening, and she was very upset to see my face so hurt. It didn't scar, but to this day I will not fry chicken. Whenever we eat it, I cook it in the oven.

I received this recipe for nut rolls from a dear neighbor, Mag Koran, who has passed on. She was always so kind to us after Mommy died and always brought these over for the holidays. I learned to make these foods from all these special women and continue to make them every year.

—*Ann Marie Krynock*

Easter Coffee Cake (nut rolls)

1 cake yeast
$\frac{1}{2}$ cup warm water
1 cup milk, scalded and cooled to lukewarm
2 eggs, beaten
2 teaspoon vanilla
4 cups flour
1 teaspoon salt
4 tablespoons sugar
1 cup Crisco

Dissolve yeast in water. Add to milk, eggs, and vanilla. Sift flour, salt, and sugar. Cut in Crisco as you would for pastry. Add liquid and beat well. Refrigerate overnight. Divide dough into 3 parts or make 4 smaller rolls. Roll each part in a long rectangle. Sprinkle with sugar and cinnamon. Then spread the nut filling (see next page) on the dough and begin rolling from one end like a jelly roll. Place on greased baking dish. Let rise for 2 hours. Brush top with beaten egg. Sprinkle with sugar and bake 30 minutes at 375°F.

FILLING

To 1-pound package of ground English walnuts add 1 to 2 cups sugar, to taste. Moisten with 2 egg whites, beaten until frothy. If needed, add a little milk to make a nice smooth paste (it shouldn't be runny).

I can remember the excitement building within my family at Easter. Mother always dyed five or six dozen eggs and we colored them and set them out on the dining room table in a large basket. After church we would line up and race through the yard looking for the eggs the rabbit stole and hid from us. We filled our baskets with eggs and toys.

Now what to do with five or six dozen eggs? Needless to say, we only ate one hard-boiled egg each—the others went into various dishes. Eggaroni was our favorite.

—*Mary Catherine Walker*

Eggaroni

2 tablespoons butter
2 tablespoons flour
Salt
3 beaten eggs
2 cups milk
3 hard-boiled eggs
2 cups elbow macaroni, cooked
½ cup celery, chopped
½ cup onion, chopped
1 cup sharp cheese, shredded (optional)

In a pan, melt butter and blend in flour. Season with salt. Beat eggs with milk and add to flour mixture. Heat to boiling point, stirring constantly.

Reserving one hard-boiled egg for garnish, in a 9-by-13 inch greased baking dish, layer macaroni, celery, onion, and hard-boiled eggs. (Occasionally she'd add 1 cup shredded sharp cheese at this point.) Pour milk-egg mixture over top. Bake at 350°F for 35 to 40 minutes. Garnish with chopped hard-boiled egg before serving.

Everyone in our family looks forward to Easter because it is the only time we make this recipe. I now have to make several because my daughters have let their friends try it and they all come looking for Cirek at Easter. This recipe was handed down to me by my mother-in-law, who received it from her mother-in-law.

—*Kathleen Dragan*

Cirek (Easter Cheese, pronounced "sidak")

12 eggs
1 quart milk
1 tablespoon salt
½ teaspoon white pepper

Pour milk into 3-to 4-quart saucepan. Break eggs into milk, one at a time. Using a rotary beater (not electric), beat eggs and milk until eggs are completely broken.

Cook over low heat, stirring constantly so mixture will not scorch. Use flat wooden paddle instead of spoon. Cook until it looks like scrambled eggs. Add salt and pepper. Pour into a strainer lined with cheesecloth. Squeeze out excess water; then tie cheesecloth tightly. Hang and let drain for several hours. Remove cheesecloth, wrap and store in the refrigerator. Serve with sliced ham on Easter.

In 1960 I was barely twenty, and moved from Shreveport, Louisiana, with my husband and six-month-old son to Rochester, New York. Needless to say, it was a true cultural shock because I had never been north of Hot Springs, Arkansas, in my life. Of course the constant cold and snow were a problem, but what I missed most after family and friends were the coffee and familiar foods.

That Thanksgiving was the first holiday that we had not spent at home and I decided that by cooking my mother's famous oyster dressing, a holiday tradition in our family, we would be less homesick. Thirty-seven years have passed and I still make it twice a year, and at other times I bake it with pork chops. I have even stuffed cabbage with it.

—*Judeth Vinson*

Oyster Dressing

2 bunches of green onions, white and green parts
1 or 2 purple onions
1 bell pepper
1 bunch celery
1 bunch parsley
2 big cloves garlic
1 stick margarine or butter
1 or 2 jars oysters and their liquid
2 eggs
1 one-pound loaf French bread, crumbled and
    lightly toasted
1 can chicken broth (may need more)
Salt, cracked red pepper, Worcestershire sauce,
    thyme, and sage

Chop the vegetables finely (I use a food processor) and sauté in the margarine or butter in a heavy Dutch oven or other large pot. Drain and coarsely chop the oysters and add them to the vegetables. Beat the eggs with a fork and stir in a little of the hot vegetable/oyster combination to prevent them from curdling in the hot pan. Add to the pot, stirring again to keep the eggs from scrambling. Add the toasted French bread crumbs and sufficient chicken broth to make a very moist mixture. Season to taste, using maybe ½ to 1 teaspoon of thyme and the tiniest little bit of sage. Put into a greased 9-by-13 inch pan and cover with foil. Bake for an hour or so with the turkey, taking the foil off for the last 15 minutes or so, so that the dressing will dry out somewhat and brown slightly.

7

Desserts

My mother was one of thirteen children, eleven of them boys. Every Saturday morning her mother would make fifteen pies to last the weekend.
—*Geraldine "Gerry" Harrison*

My father's mother was known as a great cook in the times when cooking ran to lots of butter, lard, and sugar. One of her most famous dishes was a great apple pie, a huge concoction baked in a glass dish that must have been at least three inches deep and about sixteen inches across. Seven sons made large dishes imperative. She didn't have a recipe, and never measured ingredients.

My father loved the pie and was unhappy that my mother could not cook it at home. Of course we didn't have such a magnificent pie pan anyway, and my grandmother wasn't about to share hers. But my mother did finally manage to position herself beside my grandmother once while she was making the pie, catching the handfuls of flour and sugar and spices in a measuring bowl as they came off my grandmother's hands. With her own good judgment and cooking sense, my mother, with a few experiments, managed to produce a recipe for a pie that satisfied my father, albeit reduced to a more modern and ordinary size.

My grandmother didn't think much of this slight child—it lost too much in the way of flavor because of the small size. She had a point; the huge pie took longer to bake in her old oven, and in the extra time the taste of the apples and pie dough and cinnamon deepened as the juices flowed.

But my mother's pie is one of the great treats of my childhood, one that I can reproduce, one that my own children love.

—*Wilhemina Garrison*

Mother's Version of Grandma's Extra-Delicious Apple Pie

1 cup vegetable shortening (originally lard, improved to Crisco)
3 cups flour
1 teaspoon salt
½ cup ice-cold water

For the pastry: Cut shortening into flour and salt mixture until small crumbs form. Add water a few tablespoons at a time until dough is formed. Make sure it is not too sticky. Flour board and rolling pin and roll out ½ of the dough for the bottom crust. Reserve the remaining dough for lattice top. This makes a generous amount. There may be enough left over for another single crust pie.

¼ cup butter
¼ cup flour
1¼ cups sugar

5 large cooking apples, peeled and thinly sliced (the old-style green cooking apples—hard to get now, but the best. Granny Smith may be substituted)
1 teaspoon cinnamon
1 teaspoon vanilla
½ pint heavy cream
Small marshmallows

For the filling: Cover a 9-inch pastry-lined pan with butter cut in small pieces. Sprinkle with a mixture of 2 tablespoons flour and ¼ cup sugar. On top of this place the apples and sprinkle with a mixture of cinnamon and ½ cup sugar.

Mix together 2 tablespoons flour, ½ cup sugar, vanilla, and the heavy cream. Pour over the apples, reserving three tablespoons.

Cover with a latticed crust and spread the remainder of the cream mixture over it.

Bake at 400°F for 15 minutes, then at 300°F for one hour. After pie is done, put small marshmallows in the holes of the crust and return to the oven to brown lightly.

If the edges of the pie crust are getting brown before the pie is done, cover them with strips of aluminum foil and continue baking.

Cherry pies will have a deeper cherry taste if you put a few drops of almond extract into the fruit before cooking. This works particularly well with canned cherries.

As a child, my dad grew cantaloupes, and when they were in season we enjoyed them in many different ways. For breakfast we had hot-buttered biscuits with a slice of cantaloupe. At lunch, which was our main meal, there was sliced cantaloupe to eat with our vegetables and corn bread. In the evening it was available if you chose to have another slice.

The "big treat," however, was cantaloupe pie for dessert, and there was never any left over! As far as any of us know, we are the only family that ever made or heard of cantaloupe pie. My mother came up with the following recipe.

—*Kathryn Letson*

Cantaloupe Pie

Choose a very ripe melon. Scrape the pulp from the rind (not too close unless it is very ripe). Save the juice.

1 tablespoon flour
$\frac{1}{2}$ cup sugar
2 cups (more or less) melon pulp and juice
2 eggs, beaten
4 tablespoons margarine or butter, melted

Stir together flour and sugar. Add melon pulp, juice, eggs, and butter. Pour into unbaked pie shell. Bake 45 to 50 minutes at 350°F until crust is light brown, and filling becomes slightly firm.

Very good served warm.

Never roll out a pie crust more than once. If you do it will be as tough as nails.

My grandmother, Sarah Conway, was a great cook and she made the most delicious lemon meringue pie that I've ever eaten. Whenever our family came to visit, she would make it for us, particularly for her daughter-in-law, my mother. We often sat around after dinner with two of my great aunts, ate lemon pie, played cards, or listened to the Detroit Tigers on WJR.

After Grandma's death in 1978 at the age of 100, I was given her enamel pie pan and to this day I still use it when I make a lemon pie. That pan and the pie bring back a flood of wonderful memories of my grandma.

—*Judy Conway Wilgus*

Lemon Meringue Pie

¼ cup plus ½ tablespoon shortening
¾ cup less ½ tablespoon flour
3 to 5 tablespoons ice-cold water

For the crust cut shortening into flour until it resembles coarse crumbs. Add cold water, one tablespoon at a time until soft dough is formed. Roll out on a floured board. This recipe makes a thin crust. (Never roll out more than once, or the crust will be tough.) Prick crust in several places on bottom and sides and then bake for 8 minutes in 475°F oven.

1 cup sugar
¼ heaping cup flour
¼ teaspoon salt or few sprinkles
2 or 3 eggs, separated (use the yolks for filling; save
      whites for meringue. Use 2 eggs for 8-inch pie
      plate; 3 for 9-inch pie plate)
Grated rind of 1 lemon
Juice of 1 lemon
1 cup boiling water

For the filling sift together sugar, flour, and salt. Beat yolks, and add with lemon rind and juice to flour mixture. Pour in 1 cup boiling water. Cook until thick in a double boiler, stirring all the time, about 5 to 10 minutes or longer, depending on double boiler. Pour into baked crust. (Note: Have water boiling so it just touches the bottom of the pan when you start cooking.)

2 or 3 egg whites
1/4 teaspoon cream of tartar
4 to 6 tablespoons sugar
1/3 to 1/2 teaspoon vanilla

For the meringue: Beat egg whites with cream of tartar until frothy. Add sugar 1 tablespoon at a time and beat until stiff. Pile on filling and be sure to seal edge with meringue all around. Bake 8 to 10 minutes at 400°F.

To measure a quarter cup of shortening (or any amount), put three-quarters of a cup water in your cup measure and then fill with shortening until the water rises to one cup. Drain the water and use the shortening in your recipe. This technique makes less mess and is more accurate.

Never make your mother-in-law's specialty and invite her to dinner. Mom's chocolate pound cake had been a favorite of everyone. So when we invited my mother-and father-in-law to dinner for the first time, I asked for her recipe. Well I made it, and it was about one inch high. What a flop! We all laughed and ate flat, tough chocolate cake with ice cream.
— *Susan Conway Himes*

Chocolate Pound Cake

2 sticks butter
3 cups sugar
5 eggs
3 cups flour
½ teaspoon baking powder
5 or 6 tablespoons cocoa
1 cup milk
1 teaspoon vanilla
Pinch of salt

Have ingredients at room temperature. Cream butter and sugar. Add eggs one at a time, beating after each addition. Sift together dry ingredients. Add dry ingredients and milk alternately, beginning and ending with dry ingredients. Stir in vanilla. Pour batter into a greased and floured tube pan, and bake at 325°F for 1 hour and 15 minutes.

Here's a tip: I realized after making this cake that my pan wasn't seasoned properly. Before you use it the first time, grease the bottom and sides well with shortening and put the pan into the oven. Bake 30 minutes at 325°F. Cool before you use it.

Cakes made from box mixes are much better than they used to be. Don't feel guilty using them.

If you think your baking powder is too old or no good, test it by putting a teaspoon or so in a cup of hot water. If it bubbles nicely it's okay.

Wear an apron.

Always cool cakes before frosting.

Around 1960, my mother was an editor of a cookbook published by the Omaha chapter of the National Council of Jewish Women. A writer from the women's pages of the *Omaha World Herald* did a feature story about the cookbook and the newspaper sent a photographer to get a picture of the women who had edited it.

The newspaper, however, hadn't told my mother and her coeditors that they wanted them to hold a sample dish from the cookbook, so they had nothing prepared. The article was to include the recipe for a chocolate-chip date cake, so my mother took a brown terrycloth towel, folded it up, and placed it in the cake pan.

In the days of black-and-white newspaper photography, the towel was a pretty good facsimile of a chocolate cake. But after the recipe was published, the *Omaha World Herald* received a letter from a frustrated reader. "Why didn't my cake rise as much as the cake shown in the picture?" she wrote. "Did you double the recipe?"

Thirty-five years later, we're still making this cake for family and friends—without the towel.

—*Diane Granat*

Chocolate-Chip Date Cake

1 teaspoon baking soda
1 cup dates, chopped
1 cup hot water
1 tablespoon cocoa
1½ cup flour
Pinch of salt
½ cup butter
¾ cup sugar
2 eggs

TOPPING:
½ cup chocolate chips
½ cup walnuts, chopped
2 tablespoons sugar

Sprinkle baking soda over dates and pour hot water over them. Let cool. Sift cocoa, flour, and salt together. Cream butter and sugar. Add eggs and beat well. Add sifted dry ingredients alternately with date mixture. Put into a 12-by-8-inch greased and floured pan. Mix together chocolate chips, nuts, and sugar. Sprinkle on top of cake. Bake at 325°F for 40 to 45 minutes.

Never slam a door when you have a cake or soufflé in the oven as it may fall. And never open the oven door to peek in for the same reason.

When in doubt about what to do, bake a cake.

When I was eight years old my mother asked me what kind of cake I wanted for my birthday party. I chose her cranberry coffee cake. Despite my delight, my eight-year-old friends were less than enthusiastic. Luckily a next-door neighbor joined the party and brought cupcakes with her, which saved the day.

Despite this experience, my mother's cranberry coffee cake has remained my favorite. She even mailed me a cake for my twenty-first birthday, when I was studying in Madrid. Although my mother died several years ago, my sister carries on the cranberry coffee cake tradition, often preparing it for me when I visit from out of town.

—*Jill Rosenthal*

Cranberry Coffee Cake

1 stick margarine
1 cup sugar
2 eggs
1 teaspoon baking powder
1 teaspoon baking soda
2 cups flour
½ pint sour cream
1 teaspoon almond extract
1 seven-ounce can whole cranberry sauce
½ cup walnuts

Cream margarine with sugar. Add unbeaten eggs, one at a time, and stir. Sift together baking powder, baking soda, and flour. Add dry ingredients to margarine mixture alternately with sour cream, ending with dry ingredients. Stir in almond extract. Grease and flour a tube pan. Layer half of the batter on bottom, and spread with half of the cranberry sauce. Repeat. Sprinkle with walnuts. Bake in a 350°F oven for 55 minutes.

Remove from pan after 5 to 10 minutes to cool.

Glaze with a mixture of ¾ cup confectioners' sugar, 2 tablespoons warm water, and ½ teaspoon almond extract.

If you get a piece of shell in with the egg, the easiest way to take it out is by using a piece of the empty eggshell to scoop it out.

I grew up on a small dairy farm with eighteen to twenty cows to milk twice a day. Milk was an important part of all our meals, both for drinking and cooking. One of my favorite desserts was caramel custard. It was a long time after I married before I tried to make it. I was intimidated by the caramelizing of sugar. You just could not substitute brown sugar, the taste was very different. I soon found out that an iron skillet was the secret weapon.

—*Geraldine "Gerry" Harrison*

Caramel Custard

¾ cup sugar, caramelized
1 quart warm milk
3 eggs (if small use 4)
1 tablespoon sugar
Pinch of salt

Heat sugar in an iron skillet, stirring constantly just until sugar is melted and turns a caramel color. Keep the heat low so it will not smoke. Pour the warm milk over the caramelized sugar, slowly. Simmer, stirring often, until sugar and milk are blended. Cool. Pour into lightly beaten eggs. Beat in 1 tablespoon sugar and the salt. Pour into custard cups and place cups in pan of hot water. Bake at 350°F for 40 to 50 minutes until firm.

I can still remember coming home from school—elementary, high school, college—and finding these caramels cooling on the back porch or already wrapped in little waxed paper squares. My grandmother, Bernice Belle Huffman Power, made them every Christmas, then my mother made them every Christmas until 1992. Now I make them every Christmas. They are a lot of work, but everyone in our family has always agreed they are well worth the effort.

—*Martha Siegfried Johnson*

My Mother's Caramels

5 cups white sugar
1½ sticks butter or margarine
1½ cups white corn syrup
½ teaspoon cream of tartar
5 cups milk
1 teaspoon vanilla
1 cup or more chopped English walnuts

Combine sugar, butter, corn syrup, and cream of tartar with three cups of milk and bring to boil. Add remaining milk drop by drop so boiling does not stop, stirring constantly. Cook to firm ball stage or 242°F on a candy thermometer. Add vanilla and pour into pans that have been buttered and sprinkled with walnuts. (You'll need a 9-by-13 and 9-by-9-inch pan.) When cool, cut into small pieces and wrap in waxed paper.

*It's important to make good cookies, but it's also
important how you store them. Crispy cookies like
biscotti or pizzelles should always be stored in a tin;
soft cookies can go in any old thing—from
Tupperware to a shirt box from Bloomingdale's.*

Before Christmas, Aunt Mary, Ethel Mangio, Aunt Lena, and my mother-in-law Mary would get together to make crustella, a lovely light Italian pastry. They had all come over from Italy as young children and carried on as if they were still in the old country. In some ways, they still were.

In many Italian households there would be two kitchens—the one on the first floor for "good," and the one in the basement where the real cooking took place. My mother-in-law had a linoleum floor in her basement where they'd cook, and she would always get down on her hands and knees and scrub the floor until it absolutely shone. Heaven forbid the ladies came, and there was a little dirt!

The crustellas were made out of a kind of pasta dough that Aunt Mary would roll out into very, very thin strips. Then the women would fold them into a big letter *C* and fry them. As soon as they came out of the fryer, they would pour honey and nuts over them and finish with sprinkled powdered sugar.

—*Barbara Conway Abbruzzese*

Crustellas (or crustus)

1 dozen eggs
¼ cup oil
4¼ cups flour
Honey
Chopped nuts (walnuts or pecans), optional
Powdered sugar

Beat eggs lightly. Warm oil for several minutes on stove (not too hot) and pour it into the flour. Keep working the mixture until smooth. Then add mixture to eggs, adding more flour until a smooth dough is formed. Cover. Take a piece of dough and roll thin. Cut into strips 2-inches wide and shape into a *C*. Fry in hot oil. Remove from pan and turn upside down on a wire rack. Heat honey, add nuts, and pour over the cookies. Sprinkle with powdered sugar.

To make sour milk, add one teaspoon of vinegar to one cup of regular milk.

If you're measuring some sticky liquid like honey, coat the measuring spoon with vegetable oil first. That way you get all the sticky stuff without having to stand and wait for it to drip off.

When using eggs in cooking, they should be at room temperature. If not, put them in lukewarm water for five minutes.

Always use flat, shiny cookie sheets. The brown, nonstick kind lead to burnt bottoms. Ditto cookie sheets with sides.

If you want to make chocolate-chip cookies the way mom made them when you were a kid, you have to get the *original* recipe that was on the chocolate-chip bag from way back then. They've changed it several times over the years, and not for the better.
—*Amanda Fisher*

Original Chocolate-Chip Cookies

COMBINE:
1 cup plus 2 tablespoons packed brown sugar
1 cup plus 2 tablespoons white sugar
1 cup shortening
½ cup butter
3 teaspoons vanilla

ADD:
3 eggs and blend until creamy

BEAT IN:
3¾ cup flour
1½ teaspoon baking soda
½ teaspoon salt

STIR IN:
1 cup nuts
1 twelve-ounce package chocolate chips

Drop by teaspoonfuls onto a greased cookie sheet.
Bake at 375°F for 10 minutes. Yield: 6½ dozen.

Unbaked cookie dough can be kept in the refrigerator for up to a week if well wrapped. Make the dough ahead of time and then roll it out and bake the cookies with the kids. Give them an assortment of toppings and let them create their own specialties.

8

Mom Goes Grocery Shopping
and Cleans the Kitchen

We had a large family—five kids—so grocery shopping was a big expedition in our house. Since we were a military family, it meant going to the base commissary, which was usually a huge warehouse, stocked to the gills. It wasn't unusual to see families pulling along three or four carts, loaded with food, paper products, and cigarettes.

Off we would go, every week, strung out like a line of ducklings behind my mother who knew every bargain in the place. Then it was check out, load up the station wagon, and drive home—except once, when I was left behind. I was four years old and my absence went unnoticed amidst all the groceries and kids and chaos until they pulled into the driveway, twenty miles later.

Of course, my mother turned right around and came back for me. She found me happy as can be, entertaining all the clerks behind the paymaster's counter. I was even wearing the paymaster's hat!

—*Sherry Conway Appel*

If you keep bananas in the refrigerator, the skins turn black. The inside is fine.

A few brown spots on cauliflower doesn't hurt anything. Cut them off before cooking.

When refilling the pepper shaker, put in a few whole peppercorns. They will keep the pepper flowing and add a better pepper flavor.

It's almost impossible to find decent fish at a supermarket. If you can't find a real fishmonger, ask to smell whatever they are trying to sell you. The first and most important rule is, if it smells fishy don't buy it. And look out for specials. Specials often mean they bought too much of something and it didn't sell well, so now they're dropping the price on the item to get rid of it. The problem here is, How long has it been around?

Make sure the eyes aren't sunken on a whole fish and that the gills are bright red. If you're buying a filet, have the clerk hand you the piece of fish. Using a piece of wax paper as a cover, push your thumb into it. If the flesh doesn't spring right back, it's too old. Don't be shy about telling the clerk you don't want it.

—*Cheryl Reilly*

If you're making fish stock, ask the fish clerk for any leftover heads and tails to use. Always take the gills out of the heads before you boil them.

Don't buy fish ahead of time. Buy it the same day you intend to cook it.

Rinse your hands with cold water before handling fish and they won't smell so fishy after.

They put the freshest milk on the back of the shelves at the market. This also holds true for bread, potato chips, yoghurt, and other perishable items. Don't mess up the items on the shelf, but choose from the back, especially if there's no freshness date on the package.

—*Emma Mason*

*Always clean the kitchen before starting to cook.
Never try and prepare a meal when the dishes and
utensils from the previous meal are still in the sink.*

*Clean up as you cook—you're just going to have to
do the dishes later anyway. Put the pot that needs
to be soaked in the sink with soapy water before
you serve the food. That way it will be ready to
wash when you do the rest of the dishes after
eating.*

*Never go to bed with dirty dishes in the sink. It's
just too much to face first thing in the morning.*

*Put the kitchen sponge in the dishwasher just
before turning it on.*

Even though it sounds contradictory, it only takes one-third to one-half teaspoon dried herbs to equal one teaspoon fresh.

Never go grocery shopping when you're hungry, you'll buy too much. And never go when you've just eaten, nothing looks good.

Make friends with the butcher. He'll give you better cuts of meat.

When checking out, don't look for the shortest line; go to the fastest checker. If you usually shop in the same places, you'll soon get to know which ones are fast and which ones aren't.

Rewrap cheese and cold cuts when you get home from the grocery store. They will keep much longer.

When your aluminum pots get dark inside, boil two
teaspoons of cream of tartar in one quart of water
for ten minutes to make them lighter again.

If your cutting board doesn't smell very nice, rub it
with slices of lemon or lime.

Clean your garbage disposal every once in a while by
running a tray of ice cubes through it. Grinding up a
half of a piece of citrus fruit (lemon, orange, grapefruit) also makes it smell better.

If you've burned popcorn in your microwave, help
get rid of the smell by putting some lemon pieces
and some cloves in a bowl of water and boiling for
five minutes.

The easiest way to clean cooked egg off a pan or
utensil is to use cold water, not hot.

9

Favorite Meals and Family Traditions

Our favorite meal was always roast pork with sauerkraut. My mom would cook the roast until the meat would fall off the bone at the touch of the knife. Still, the meat was always moist. Then she would take the roast out and let it sit while she stirred the sauerkraut in the roast pan with the drippings from the meat. We had to have mashed potatoes and peas with this meal, or it just didn't come out right. On your plate you put a chunk of pork (the crispy outside if you could get it) and a pile of potatoes with the sauerkraut right on top. Off to the side was as few green peas as you could get away with.

It was very important to eat the sauerkraut

mixed in with the mashed potatoes. I can't imagine eating it any other way.

—*Sandy Fisher*

My mother has told us this story so often it has become family legend. A friend was preparing dinner when my mother came in and found her sawing about three inches off the small end of a ham. She was using a hacksaw to cut through the bone. Mom asked her why she was doing that and she said, "Because my mother always did it this way." On further questioning it became clear that the friend didn't know why she did it; it was just the way it was always done in her family.

A few weeks later the friend called Mom up and said her mother had been to visit. She asked her why she always cut three inches off the small end of a ham. Her mother told her it was the only way she could fit it into the pan she cooked the ham in!

—*Sunday Wynkoop*

Buy the best knives you can afford. You don't need many, but the ones you have should always be kept sharp. You'll cut yourself more times with a dull knife than a sharp one.

Never soak your good knives or put them in the dishwasher.

Mother was raised in the oil fields just after the turn of the century. As soon as she could, she left for the city and left all that she could behind her . . . but she couldn't leave the apple dumplings. We had them every year, just as soon as the early transparent apples began to fall in mid-July. This is poor person's food: we serve dumplings for Saturday lunch for twelve or more guests and never spend more than ten dollars for the entire meal.

—*Frannie Fisher*

Lois's Apple Dumplings

2 cups milk
½ cup brown sugar
2 baking apples
1 cup white-bleached, enriched flour
2 teaspoons baking powder
Cinnamon to taste
Brown sugar to taste

First, mix milk with brown sugar in a serving pitcher. Set aside. Pare and cube two apples. Sprinkle with a little brown sugar. Mix 1 cup flour with baking powder (Royal brand, if you can get it). Add enough whole milk to make a soft dough. Flour the board. Roll the dough to ½-inch thickness. Cut into three triangles. Fill each with the apples and plenty of cinnamon and more brown sugar. Close tight and drop into unsalted boiling water. Cover and boil for 15 minutes. They'll be grapefruit-size.

Serve in a cereal bowl. Open the dumpling with your spoon and fill with the sweetened milk. Don't serve kids more than one (they might explode!).

I was in college at the University of Maryland, sitting one night in an all-girl dorm, talking about food. I was bragging about how my parents were European and that I had eaten artichokes from when I was a small child. One of my dorm roommates, Marge Fuzo, asked me how I had eaten them.

"Of course, we always dipped the leaves in catsup," I told her proudly.

My mother died when I was really young. But I still have this memory of a steamed artichoke on the table and a bowl of catsup. We kids loved it that way!

—*Annie Groer*

When I was growing up, my parents lived with my mother's parents. My grandmother and then later my mother made the best vegetable soup. I liked to eat it in the morning before going off to school since I wasn't much of a fan of cereal.

When I married and wanted to make the soup, I had to watch my mother make it so I could learn how. I have made this soup many times over the twenty-nine years of my married life and my daughter is always happy to have me bring her a quart or so when I visit her family or to make it for her. It always tastes good.

—*Darleen Foster*

Vegetable Soup

Cook soup bones covered with water, salt, pepper, and onion for a couple hours to make the beef stock. (Let that get cold and skim off the fat.) You can also use canned beef broth and boullion cubes to make about 2 quarts.

To beef stock, add 1 large onion, 3 stalks celery, 1 green pepper, 2 carrots, ½ head of cabbage, all cut into small pieces. Add one cup Lima beans. Let simmer for about ten minutes, then add 1 large sweet potato, 2 white potatoes, both types potatoes cut into half-inch cubes, 1 diced turnip, 1 cup corn, and ½ cup alphabet pasta. When the vegetables have all fully cooked, add one quart tomato juice. Bring soup back to a simmer and serve.

As children, we were always delighted to find the metal mixing bowl and beaters chilling in the refrigerator. We knew that lemon sherbet would be coming as a special summertime treat. In 1978, when my husband and I were stationed in California and Mother came to visit, we made sherbet from the lemons from our own tree. It had been so hot that the lemons were almost cooking outside so we made as much sherbet as we could so as few lemons would go to waste as possible. Mom's lemon sherbet always brings back sweet childhood memories, so it's no wonder it's a favorite dessert.

Limes can be substituted for lemons in this recipe. When using limes, though, you add less sugar because limes are sweeter than lemons. This recipe makes about one and a half pints. You serve much less sherbet than ice cream because it is so sweet.

—Kathleen McDuffie

Lemon Sherbet

1¼ cups sugar
⅓ cup lemon juice
Grated rind of one lemon
¼ teaspoon lemon extract
1 pint (2 cups) milk (whole or 2 percent)

Combine sugar, lemon juice, rind, and lemon extract. Stir well. Add milk slowly, while stirring. Stir until the sugar is dissolved. Pour into ice cube trays (the kind without the cube dividers), pie pan, or other shallow container. Place pan in the freezer until firm but not solid. Remove from freezer and place into a chilled metal mixing bowl. Beat with chilled beaters until mixture is light and creamy. Return to freezing tray and place in the freezer. Stir once with a spoon after freezing a short while. After sherbet is totally frozen, scoop into a covered container.

Your Recipes

Here is the most important part of the book. This is where you pass along your special recipes and thoughts, or where you ask your mom to give you hers. This is forever.

———————— ———————— ————————

———————— ———————— ————————

———————— ———————— ————

———————— ————

———————— ——

————————————————————————

————————————————————————

Acknowledgments

$\mathcal{I}$ would like to thank these very special women—mothers, daughters, aunts, grandmothers, friends—who shared their special memories with me. Their stories and recipes truly show that the kitchen is where you find the heart of the family. We are all fortunate to have these bits of our past to share with those who will carry on these traditions into the next century. Many, many thanks to each of you:

Barbara Conway Abbruzzese, Mary Abbruzzese; Irene Trippett Appel, Sandy Appel Fisher, Amanda Frederickson; Pam Beer, June F. Beer; Stephanie Benkovic, Carolyn Benkovic; Karen Bloomfield; Nancy L. Blush; Loretta Booth, Emma Mason;

Elizabeth Force Carson, Patricia L. Force; Peggy Cavender, Effie Violet Jordan Cavender; Ann Cochran, Grace Peters Sanfilippo; Penny Cooper; Ruth Rice Crone, Carolyn Crone; Mary Dail, Neva Gan Weeks; Lennie Doak, Susan Doak; Susan Dotchin, Sarah Duckworth, Lula Huxham; Kathleen Dragan, Barbara Kopcak Dragan; Kathleen Ewing, Joanne Ewing; Annie Felts, Sarah Felts; Jane Carolyn Fleming, Dorothy V. Fleming, Anne Fleming Ridgely; Frannie Fisher, Lois Fisher; Darlene Foster, Fae Richards Walton, Esther Gemeny Richards; Sally McCoy Games, Betsy Games McCord, Peggy Hale McCoy; Wilhemina Garrison; Diane Granat, Edith Granat; Annie Groer, Hannah Kessler Groer; Lynn Gutter, Carole Gutter, Sophie Silverman; Geraldine "Gerry" Harrison, Linnie Faber Vickers; Nancy Fissel Hauser, Dorothy Fissel; Sue Henyon, Amanda Buckwalter; Susan Conway Himes, Julie Himes Gerig, Estelle Forshaw Himes; Martha Siegfried Johnson, Mary Myrtle Power Siegfried, Bernice Belle Huffman Power; Terry Jones, Ho Po-Lan; Jane G. Kelly; Rabia Khan, Razia Durrani; Sandra Kidwell; Ann Marie Krynock, Helen Mazur, Mary Monak, Julia Butchko,

Mag Koran; Kathryn Letson, Ari Etta Herrod; Reann Lydick, Ida Vertner Beaver Joseph, Sallie Ruth Joseph Church, Judith Ann Church Lydick; Karyn Lynch, Dorothy Lynch; Liz McClain, Edith Lesser, Sarah Miller; Kathleen McDuffie, Mae O'Connor; Barbara Dawson Marcinko, Martha Dawson; Linda O'Connor, Marilyn Schwab; Kay Dietmeyer Opeka, Dorothy Dietmeyer York; Margie Polk, Grace Burkey; Ruth E. Pope; Cina Radler, Harriet Radler; Sally Reister, Carol Kidner; Jill Rosenthal, Joyce Karp Lindmark; Anna Rae Ruckman, Stella Katchan Wheeler; Amelia Santacroce, Grace Martino, Mary Pantalena, Jane Defourneaux; Judy Schoder; Lois Shaw, Beth Hanner; Beverly Silverberg, Anne Gubenko Rabner, Nina Silverberg; Martha Stauber; Ruthann Stone, Athelia Rupp; Eileen Toumonoff, Louise Thoron MacVeagh; Judeth Vinson, Ethel Banner Gaignard; Mary Catherine Walker, Mary Lou Nemir; Judy Conway Wilgus, Helen Keyzer Conway, Sarah Sevier Conway, Anna Sevier Facey; Sabrina Williams, Geneva Woodard, Ethlyn Knowles; Jennifer Wingard, Charlotte Wingard; Sunday Wynkoop, Susan Hammett.

Index